ECHOES OF THE BLEEDING HEART

SONALI SINHA

to my parents and my siblings.

Contents

Contents

Contents

Preface

This book will introduce you to the world of poems and a beautiful serenity.

So this didn't happen all of a sudden but it's just a series of the chaotic experiences which pushed me towards the beautiful world of poetry.

Escaping from the reality I found solace in poems and i think it brings peace to everyone's life.

I want you to introduce to my little world of chaos and poems.

hoping for the best.

Acknowledgements

Gratitude for everything.

Thanking the universe, mahadev for this particular moment.

I feel like ocean of words are floating in my heart for expressing the gratitude to each and every person in my life but still it can't be expressed just in a single piece of paper.

Thanks.

1. Heart or art?

Her heart,
slit into pieces,
every drop of blood
which fell down
bloomed into a flower.
Broken things
turn into beautiful art pieces,
her heart,
was an astounding illustration of that.
The dagger
perfectly did its work,
and turned her heart
into a treasure.
Not only blood,
it pumped dreams
for her.
The dream like flowers
were supplied
with her blood
to grow,
to bloom.

2. A day dreamer girl

The blood
was dripping off
her shoulders,
the knife,
all covered in blood.
Her curls drenched
in sweat,
and finding their ways
in between her eyes.
The dried crimson eyes
suspected deception.
Deception
from her own self,
the way
she throttled
her myriad dreams
by her own quivering hands,
she was drowning in her own tears and blood.
The blood was seeping
from the bruises
of a day dreamer girl.

3. From the grave

Once again
the grave of my tears
is howling,
and seeking
for the answers,
I'm asphyxiating,
and crawling
to reach the door,
but the weight of the queries,
is dragging me towards the grave.
call me craven
because I lack the responses,
I'm capitulating
and going
their way,
I wish
to witness my interment
along with my tears.

4. Hues of the dreams

Write your dreams with the red ink,
and the details of the obstacles in the pink.
Black would represent the worst days,
green is good for hopeful rays.
Your smile would be painted in blue,
tell me about the violets if you have any clue.
Saffron would signify about your love,
and eyes would be full of stars above.
Grey is for days full of illusions,
Olive may portray about your confusions.
Adhere the torn pages with white glue,
and fulfill your dreams with beautiful hues.

5. Nightmares

Clutching the sheets too tight,
when will she overcome this night.
Trying to scream but unable to do so,
escaping from something but where would she go.
Throbbing and sweating profusely,
the happenings were very obstruesly.
stuck with a closed entrance,
and her mind full of repentance.
that was an eerie nightmare,
a day dreamer girl wanted to share.

6. Autumn

That new born hapless flower
is celebrating the autumn,
each leaf is narrating a different story of life
and prognosticating
about the afterlife
to the new guests.
The epitome of tranquility
after falling down
is enchanting according to those deceased beautiful leaves.
They are accompanying
the decaying days and nights,
reaching their graveyard
and sharing their beauty
with the world.
The setting sun,
the raising moon,
the falling stars,
witnessing
the arrival of the autumn.

7. Phoenix

Gathering her ashes
she is the phoenix,
she belongs
to the world of beautiful hues of love,
accompanied by the shadows
of the the chaos
which she hides
in the blink of her eyes,
she will rise
with the palette of pain and fire.

8. Tell the world

Tell the world,
that I was not valorous.
Tell the world,
that I lost a war
with myself.
Tell the world,
that I could not pick up the sword
to kill my own demons.
Tell the world,
that I entered hellscape
and never found my home again.
Tell the world,
that I became a chimera,
that too in love.
Tell the world,
that I was so capacious,
I held the ocean of agony inside me.
Tell the world,
that I lost a war.

9. The cursed fortress

The folklores
I heard in my childhood
that the cursed fortresses
had graves of reminiscences.
I have become
one
of
them.
Not less than a fortress
my heart is,
it has consumed
the recollections of the miseries.
The graves
of those reminiscences
echo in the lap of hushed nights
and gets stabbed
by the sunbeams.
For I too,
waiting to be stabbed
and burst out blood and miseries.

10. Glorious wounds

Beneath that facade
the agonizing heart
ready to avenge its monsters.
This time is for glory,
all the bruises left open
to bleed,
to remember all the torments,
to remember all the anguishes,
to realise all the ambushses.
Turning all the afflicts into a sword,
it will invade,
it will win,
not that soon
but certainly
in this very lifespan.

11. Not a bad dream

Perhaps that was not a bad dream,
no, I did not want to scream.
I did not go
to collect the withered flowers,
I did not wait for him
hours and hours.
Neither I noticed the birds
returning their nest,
nor I saw when the sun
traversed to the west.
I was never waiting for the moon,
I did not want to go home too soon.

12. Her madness

If she'll tell you about
what's going on
inside her mind,
you'll consider her mad.
So she turns her madness into poetry
and her poetry into madness.

13. The dusk

The dusk
entered in her balcony
with a few pieces of stars
along with it.
The blue sky
now started turning into a dark one.
She was losing herself
in the serenity of darkness,
now the moon didn't seem so far
but not even so eminent,
the suffocating one needs only this calmness
and solace of the darkest hours.

14. Girl from the ocean

Boy from the dreams

I'm your girl from the ocean,

you have stars in your eyes

and I've your dreams in my eyes.

Let's hide behind the clouds,

so none can see us

getting lost in each other.

Let's meet at the dusk

or the dawn

forgetting about the brighter world

and the darkness.

There's a magic when your eyes meet mine

and when you look at me like there's nothing else in the world

to look at,

the neverending love poems,

the beautiful words of love songs,

reminds me of you.

15. The last stroke

That
was the last stroke
and she
completed her painting.
She cannot remember,
how many nightmares it took
to pick up the paint brush
and dip into her own blood
to create that masterpiece.
The howl of her soul
echoed in her ears
yearning to complete
that unfinished painting.
She revived her bleeding wounds
in despair
and tormented her bruises
again and again
just for that masterstroke.

16. You

I'm not desiring
for any rosebed,
neither I'm demanding
for the whole sky,
nor for the constellations.
Denying for the luxuriant artefacts,
defying the whole world,
My fingers are refusing
for those exquisite stones,
I seek
one promise
which is just.
One promise
over everything.
If you
my beloved
swear to stay with me
till the day
I become detritus.

17. Siesta

I am in siesta,

wandering

in an etheral world.

No, don't wake me up,

as I don't want to exist there,

why it feels

someone is staring at me,

suffocating me

and choking me.

Now I feel breathlessness,

The world is shrinking,

the hope is fading.

The ashes

of the pyre

of my desire

is clogging up all the ways I can inhale.

Now this tale would be unfinished,

and the characters would be arcane.

18. Saviour

You are seeking for the answers
which reside in you,
engulf the sorrow,
and break this queue.
They will never allow you
to chase you dreams,
Move further,
it is not as excruciating as it seems.
They may fumble
but keep your rage burning in your heart,
don't let it turn into ashes
until it forms into an art.
They since an perpetuity
waiting for your failure,
choke them with your triumph
be your own saviour.

19. A prisoner

She
is scuffling
with herself,
her hope,
her determination
is shackled.
She
is a prisoner
of her own thoughts.
The veil
of the world
is torn apart,
and the whispers
of her subconsciousness
is turning true.
The rope stains
on her soul
is turning blue.
She is counting her wounds
with her bleeding fingers.
Then her silent screams vowed,
that they will succumb
in front of her.

20. I lost my wings

I lost my wings
somewhere in the ocean,
while I was drowning.
The rush
to save myself
led my wings
to vanish in the waters.
Yes,
I was flapping in the air
when I fell from the brink of my expectations.
Then I was searching
for my wounded wings,
they must have been
dissected by the the creatures residing there.
Their flesh must have been
eaten up by the fishes and otters.
The ocean must have been
turned crimson
by swallowing my wings.

21. I owe a tear drop

I owe
a tear drop
to the clouds,
when my dried eyes
felt a lack of water,
they whined to the clouds.
After all the curtains
of my feeble eyes
soaked the tears,
I felt an inadequacy of one.
One.
Just one.
So I borrowed
from the clouds.
I owe
a tear drop
to the clouds.

22. Gravestone

I plucked
the flowers,
I picked up my heart,
with my bare hands.
My tender heart,
reciting a ballad
while transforming into a gravestone.
I gathered
all the emotions
scattered all around.
Ah, the futile emotions
lost their shelter.
Now,
the nighthawks reside
in that deserted heart.

23. Self made universse

She is an inhabitant
of a self made universe,
the moon and the stars
reside in her purse.

24. An abandoned house

That was an abandoned house
surrounded by wildflowers and thorns
immersed in the shadows of tranquility.
Birds rarely taken shelter there during the cloud burst,
the path leading to it
was somewhat collapsed
and hindered by sudden obstacles,
then how did you manage to step here.
And those cracks in the walls
which always looked scary to her,
now turned illuminant
having light rays passing through it
and comforting the soul.
Then the only persistent thing
was the wildfllower
and her love for them.

25. Dew drops

• 25 •

And the ocean
feels lack of tears to cry,
the atmosphere
gasps for more air,
those neverending roads
wait in silence
for their destinations,
the morning wails
and we call those tears
as dew drops.

26. Rose petals

Her heart began to palpitate
when she observed him so close,
and in her favourite diary
she kept the petals of his rose

27. I belong to the sky

• 27 •

Let me merge
into the blues of the sky
for I always belonged to the sky.
When the clouds will downpour
their heaviness,
my tears will help them
in doing so.
I will follow the storms
till I lose my wrath
and devour my thunder.
I will walk
on the stardust
till my pondering heart
stops chasing the rainbow.
I will burn
in the sunshine
till my rage
turn into ashes.

28. Torn pages

She

is a neverending storybook.

The pages,

which describe about her dreams

are torn.

She

will write

about her dreams

along with her nightmares,

with her blood turned ink.

29. Lost hope

Every page felt blank then,
and every character
just vanished,
she couldn't find the initials of the story.
Everything was illusion,
she was just hallucinating in love,
and every lost hope was phantasm,
then she bled poems,
inhaled the words,
and covered the bruises with the poems.
The more deep were the bruises,
the more beautiful the poems,
so she kept bleeding poetry.

30. Aftermath

Wrote verses and verses
with a thought
to complete
writing you,
my beloved.
Still in between,
still in oblivion,
then I wrote pages and pages
with the same thought
to complete
writing you
my beloved.
Still the ink seems insufficient
and my heart wrenched.
So, I am writing lot and a lot
with the very same notion
to complete
writing you
my beloved.
Afterall,
you are my aftermath,
my beloved nightmares.

31. Her cloudy eyes

• 31 •

Surely her cloudy eyes
are devoid of stars,
but they downpour
the immense love for him,
And his eyes are
a pair of constellations,
she'll burn herself
but never let his light dim.

32. Poetry for you

Every moment when the sun rays
touch the surface of the earth,
I'll write a poetry for you.
Whenever birds will go to their nest
from near our balcony,
I'll write a poetry for you.
Every time when you'll stare at me
while during stargazing,
I'll write a poetry for you.
When the rain droplets will make strings of jewels
on the street wires,
I'll write a poetry for you.
When the gust of wind will open the window panes
and will bring your fragrances,
I'll write a poetry for you.
And each moment
when the sun ray will depart from our room
leaving a beautiful dusk behind,
I'll write a poetry for you.

33. This is how it begins

Putting ocean of emotions
on the paper
including all the ornamental words,
that's how poetry begins.
May be true,
may be not,
poetry is sky
poetry is sleepless nights and dull days,
poetry is life and demise,
poetry is a beautiful smile wrapped in a lot of tears,
poetry doesn't have a start or an end,
it's just a part of us,
poetry is dusk,
poetry is love,
love is poetry,
poetry is dawn.

34. Home

These miles of gaps
between us
is filled with the poems,
a lot of love poems.
When I write a poem for you,
I approach towards you one step closer
and as you recite my poetry,
eventually you proceed towards me.
This is the way I meet you
through my poems,
this is the way
we find our home.

35. Unsent letters

The nightmare of abrupt change
takes the breath away,
it's more like a part of the soul is captured
at a very serene place
but getting suffocated there
and every dead leaf
yearning to touch the ground
but taken away somewhere else
by the wind,
the unfinished storybook
is agonizing to share its not so happy ending with me
and the path of dead end, welcoming its travellers very
beautifully.
The words from the letter
inside that ivory coloured envelope is trying hard
to narrate its story,
the mystical pen bled,
consumed the pain and turned it into the most beautiful tale.

36. That closed window

The closed window
I was staring at,
was draped in the layers of dust.
Some herbs were trying
to enter into the room
through the broken glass panes,
sun rays
making its way
through the cracks of the window
to go inside,
but reflected back by the closed doors.
The books on the shelf,
staring at the strangers
passing by that house,
the happenings of the past
were yearning to the journeyers
to be a listener of their grievous tales.
The closed window
was now moving away
from my eyes
after narrating its heart out.

37. Eternity

The question of purpose of my existence

leads me

to you.

I fear

if you really are

my destination,

my morbid eyes are sick of looking at everything

but you.

I exist

for a pair of eyes

to gaze at me

for eternity.

38. The sunshine

The gust of air
forcibly opened the window panes,
the golden hues of sun rays
met her brown eyes,
the rays got reflected
by the walls of her room
witnessing a glorious entrance.
Then the wind chimes
broke the silence
and filled the surrounding with mellifluous sounds,
the strong fragrance of coffee
spread in the air,
and there she was,
ready with her ink
to give birth to a new poetry.

39. Ecstasy

Staring at the birds lost in ecstasy
thinking about how they would have reached home,
dreaming and finding my disoriented self in fantasy
and waiting for my dreams to blossom,
touching the clouds and flapping everywhere
spreading the ink on the blank page,
penning down the love that how much I care
so I completed the letter before it's haze,
though they know the path of their shelter
but do they find their momentarily niche so high,
sprinkling the epiphany in every letter
sending him letters while looking at the sky.
Finally the birds reached home and my letters in his hands,
he must have read them just at a glance.

40. Daffodils

Each ray floret
of the graceful daisy
appeared wilted,
she took a glance
at the dried bushes,
wizened twigs
and much more,
the creaky garden
felt like a cursed place,
wanted to wake up from the nightmare,
wanted to go out of the haunted garden,
but,
never woke up,
captured and trapped
by the captivating daffodils.

41. Falling for the ocean

• 41 •

Falling for the ocean
even after knowing about the menace
it holds for her,
the gravity of its superficial sublimity will lead her
to an extra beautiful world of pearl oysters,
but,
after drowning her to peace,
even after being aware
falling for the ocean.

42. The conqueror

• 42 •

She will conquer
all her nightmares
and dreams that would never decease,
turning all her anguishes into poetry
she will emerge like a masterpiece.

43. The lost shelter

That beautiful bird
trying to find her shelter,
the day was tiring for her,
her family must be waiting.
An endearing little nest
not just twigs or leaves
but made up of
a lot and a lots of love.
Her tiny babies must be waiting
to be fed by mumma.
Same surroundings,
same sunshine,
but not the very same conditions,
she found her nest
but in pieces.
She screamed,
sadly not so loud for the sapiens.

44. To your town

• 44 •

I'll paint the flowers for you
and bring the pretty clouds down,
If you affirm my poems
I'll come with the stars to your town.

45. The screams

It is not over,
it is not as uncomplicated
as it seems to be,
there are still boundaries,
there are still shackles,
they are still caged.
Can't even call you sightless,
if you see the whole world but their plight.
Can't even call you affectless,
if you hear the whole world but their screams.
They are confronting the world,
it will end them
or their shrieks.

46. My moon

There's a fear
of losing you,
there's a calmness
in getting you.
No matter how many times
they try to sabotage us,
we'll rebuilt ourselves
in front of them,
you my moon
if promise
to never relinquish me.
We may stumble
on our path,
but never dupe
the end of our journey.

47. Fire within me

Only way
to quench this thirst
is to swallow the fire,
stuck in my throat.
If I spew out this fire
instead of engulfing
then the world may burn in love,
the stars may crumble,
the moon may vow,
so I choose
to gulp down
this ocean of fire

48. My blood is blue

I drink water
from the thunder,
the storm inside me
often makes them wonder.
My blood is blue
I swallow the dark clouds,
whenever my tears turn into pearls
then all the illusion applauds.
I prick my bruises
and cure them with the hurricanes,
gathering my strength
I break all the chains.

49. The moon and the pole star

Among various constellations, galaxies and asteroids,
the moon chose me as his pole star.
The moon
never remains same,
always goes through the phases
on the contrary,
the pole star
never changes even its position.
Inspite of being aware about the moon,
the pole star chose to remain at a perfect place
and gaze
at the moon,
even when the moon disappears.
This is how
the pole star keeps falling in love
with the moon.

50. Stardust

I wish to fly high
with my broken wings,
and want to roam around
where the nighthawk sings.
The heart desires to collect the stardust
with my shivering hands,
and wander in the cosmos
where the aglow sunshine lands.
I wish to bring the pearls
with my drowning determination,
I want to burn in the warmth of the moon
and not just in infatuation.

51. Wreath of thorns

I would but smile
if eyes not filled with tears of joy,
but this cycle persists,
the wreath of thorns
squashes my throat,
words knocking at the door
but everything seems apathetic for me.

52. Wildflowers

If you ever wish
to meet her,
please bring a bunch of wildflowers
along with you,
and a Tulip
for the girl who looked like a Daisy,
she always liked wildflowers much.
She climbed the hills
and hurt herself
a number of times
just to collect those wildflowers.
And now
their aroma
surrounds her grave after everyone left.
So if you ever wish
to meet her,
please bring wildflowers
along with you.

53. My diary

The walls are haunting me
and my diary is taunting me,
now my window often says
that it can't allow the sun rays,
the flowers are now wilted
the painting wants to stay tilted,
my heart always screams
why I'm wandering in the dreams?

54. Illusion

I don't know
where is the line
which separates illusions
and the reality,
I sometimes
contemplate illusions as reality,
and reality as illusion.
I find solace
in the reality of illusions
and often I get slammed
by the reality,
for I want to be there forever
where you exist
doesn't matter,
if it's reality or illusion.

55. Aching heart

I did not want to
but still,
I woke up
with my aching heart,
as because
I found you
in the places
to which I was not a part of,
I really wanted
to slit my throat
and pen down a poetry for you
with my blood,
but I was intoxicated
with your thoughts
and slept again,
to have your dreams.

56. Her broken smile

She was smiling
like a rainbow after the cloudburst,
the broken yet beautiful smile she had.
It took to break her own heart
to smile like that,
it took a zillion of torments
to smile like that,
it took her to burn in the agony
to smile like that,
and it took her to bury herself
in her own flesh
to smile like that.

57. Rainbow

High sky is her home
she flies there with her wounded feathers
embracing all her flaws and scars,
sometimes writing sonnet
on the clouds,
and sometimes colouring her tears in his favourite hues,
sometimes touching the ambrosia and sometimes getting
drenched in the rain,
sometimes playing with the hurricanes and sometimes
fighting with the wind,
she sees the exquisite moment
when his sunshine meets her rain droplets
and create a glorious rainbow.

58. While closing her eyes

The beautiful flickering lights were going far away from her
or may be she was approaching the opposite way.
The shimmering stars started fading,
all she can see was a blurry illusion,
illusion of thoughts,
illusion of promises,
illusion of togetherness,.
The world out there
while closing her eyes
was mesmerizing,
and all her grief went away,
every misery faded,
each wound healed,
while closing her eyes.

59. The cowardice

The curtains swallowed the sunshine
entering through my window,
the darkness conquered my shelter again,
I inhaled
and filled my lungs with the gloomy air,
as it felt better than getting choked.
The demons in the next corner of my room
started wailing
along with the howling wolves
the shadows on the walls got darker and darker.
I was once again
got surrounded by the defeatism,
I was petrified meanwhile grasping the sheets.
I just gasped
and waited for the next morning
as may be I could get out of this cowardice,
gather some fortitude and confront.

60. An uninhabited castle

I don't have a story
my worthless tears ate it all up,
every character just vanished,
all the footsteps disappeared,
and my heart became an uninhabited castle.

61. The grief

How can you do this?
No, I can't answer you.
You're telling me
to share my sorrow,
that's a very tragic thing.
Sorrow resided in my heart
when everybody wanted to depart.
Grief was the only thing,
which lasted all the spring.
It kept me alive,
when I did not even wish to survive.
So tell me how can I share the most important thing
of my life?

Chapter 62

The heaviness inside me
started conquering my dreams,
the dreams in which I preserved you.
The demonic figures of my room
scratched the edges of my bed while trying to reach me.
I quickly closed my eyes,
clutched the pillows,
exhaled my fear,
and confronted.
I confronted.
I won.
I regained the lost hope.

Chapter63

For me he never loses
his eyes are full of hope,
I don't remember how he hid his tears
and how he managed to cope.

I plucked
    the flowers,
    I picked up my heart,
    with my bare hands.
    My tender heart,
    reciting a ballad
    while transforming into a gravestone.
    I gathered
    all the emotions
    scattered all around.
    Ah, the futile emotions
    lost their shelter.
    Now,
    the nighthawks reside
    in that deserted heart.

www.ingramcontent.com/pod-product-compliance
Lightning Source LLC
Chambersburg PA
CBHW031503150726
47990CB00007B/2851